Tony Hart

PRINTING & PATTERNS

A fun BOOK

Kaye & Ward · Kingswood

BLOCK PRINTS

Cut a pattern from card.
You can make a small
picture from card shapes
like the one shown here,
or make a pattern from
squares and circles, etc.

Stick your pattern together onto a wooden block or a piece of card.

If you stick your pattern to card, cut around the design and press a lump of Plasticine to the back.

Paint the printing block with poster paint or powder paint. Add a little washing-up liquid to stop the paint from drying too quickly. Press the block onto a sheet of paper.

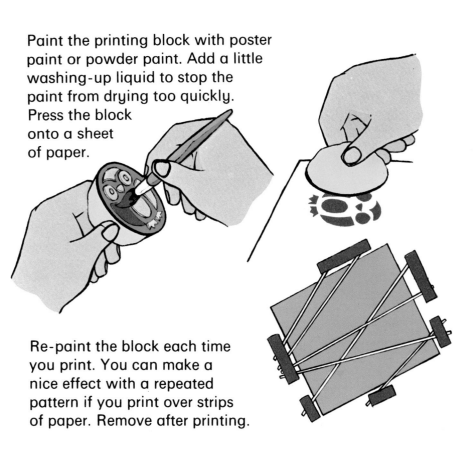

Re-paint the block each time you print. You can make a nice effect with a repeated pattern if you print over strips of paper. Remove after printing.

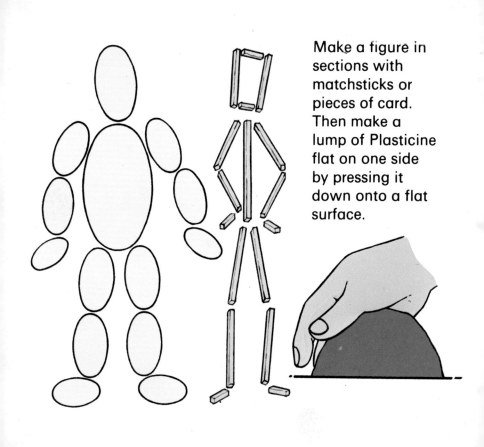

Make a figure in sections with matchsticks or pieces of card. Then make a lump of Plasticine flat on one side by pressing it down onto a flat surface.

Trim the edge of the Plasticine to a rectangular shape. Press the pieces of card or matchsticks into the flat surface.

Make a print by painting the block in the same way as in 'block printing'. Move an arm or a leg between each print.

With these movable prints you can make an animated picture. Cut two strips of paper twice as wide as your block.

Make a print on each by lining up the block with the edge of the paper. Make the figure move as shown for the second sheet.
Staple the two pieces together. Flip the top piece up and down and your figure will move. Now make more action pictures for a flip book.

EDGE PRINTS

Paint the edge of a piece of card and press it onto a sheet of paper. Try using different types of card, e.g. corrugated for a different effect.

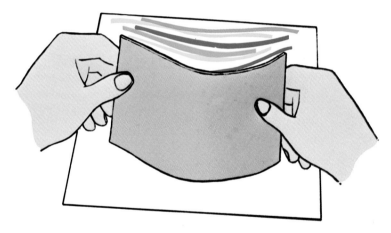

Bend the card to make curves, or fold it to make angles. You can print rectangles from the end of a matchbox, or circles from bottle tops.

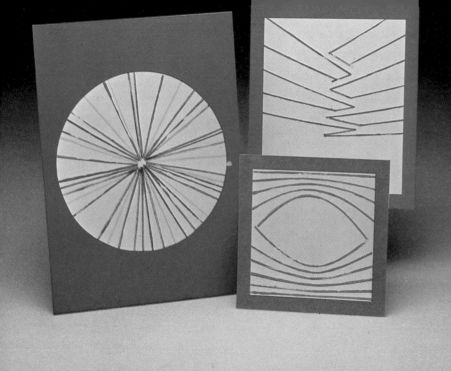

TRANSFER AND MONO PRINTS

Squeeze about one inch of water-based printing ink onto a flat surface such as Formica. Roll out the ink with a roller to an even film.

Draw a picture or cut one out from a magazine.
To make your monoprint put a piece of clean paper
over the film of ink. Place the picture on top and
trace over it in pencil.

You can rub in
areas of shading
with your finger.
Now lift off the
finished print.

For transfer prints roll out the ink
as before and draw a picture
or pattern into the ink film.

Make patterns with a pencil, pieces of card or
anything that will remove or scrape away the ink.
You can even try dabbing the ink with a sponge.

Carefully place a sheet of paper over your
design. Hold it in place with one hand
and rub over it with a soft cloth.
Lift off the paper.

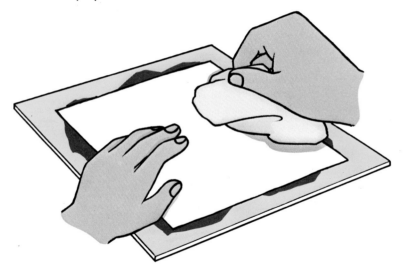

Try making prints with two or
more colours together.

FINGER PRINTS

Press your fingers onto the inked flat surface and then onto paper. Make patterns, animals and figures by adding a few pen lines.

Use strips of paper to mask out areas. You can also make patterns with the roller. Just ink it up and see what designs you can make.

WAX TRANSFER

Rub a wax crayon over some greaseproof
paper. Use several different colours.

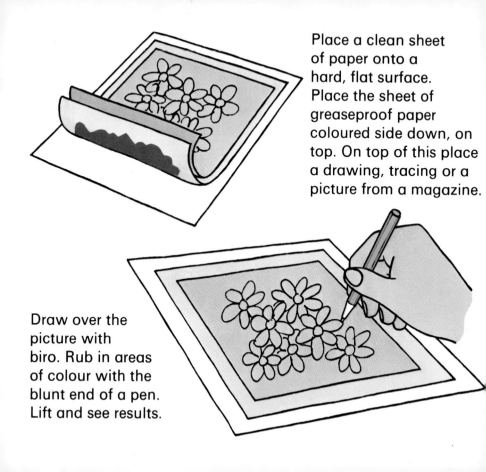

Place a clean sheet of paper onto a hard, flat surface. Place the sheet of greaseproof paper coloured side down, on top. On top of this place a drawing, tracing or a picture from a magazine.

Draw over the picture with biro. Rub in areas of colour with the blunt end of a pen. Lift and see results.

You can also cover the greaseproof paper with a white wax crayon. Make your drawing, then paint the paper with a sponge.

Where you have pressed through the paper the transferred wax will not be coloured by the paint.

MASKS AND STENCILS

Fold a piece of card in half and cut out a shape or design.

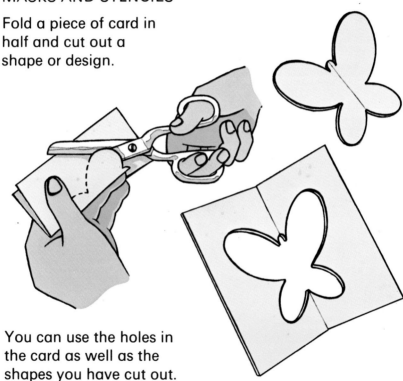

You can use the holes in the card as well as the shapes you have cut out.

You can make a picture in a number of different ways. Dip the bristles of a toothbrush into some paint. Flick the bristles with your thumb.

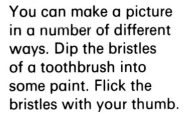

Or use a piece of sponge to dab the paint on. Use powder paint or make chalk dust with chalk and sandpaper and apply with a pad of cotton wool.

SCREEN PRINTING

Screen printing is another way of using masks. Pin a piece of net curtain to a piece of plywood or cork tile.

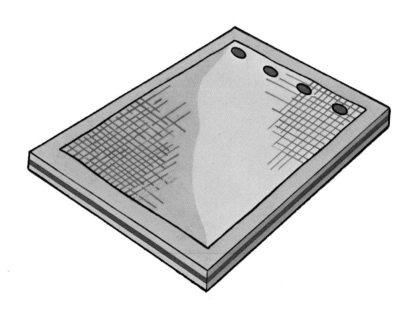

Make a pattern on the screen by sticking shapes cut from sticky back plastic onto the other side of the screen, or by painting a picture with PVA glue. Put a sheet of plastic under the screen before you paint on the glue. Do not remove it until the glue is dry.

Mask off all areas where you do not want the paint to go through.

You can make your screen print by dabbing on paint with a sponge or flicking paint with a toothbrush. Or you can squeeze out water-based printing ink along the top of the screen and spread the ink down towards you with a stiff card.

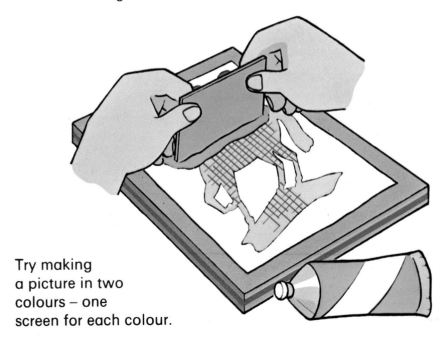

Try making a picture in two colours – one screen for each colour.

Designed by Charles Mills
Produced by Stuart Fiddes and Carnan House

First published by

Kaye & Ward Ltd
The Windmill Press
Kingswood
Tadworth, Surrey

ISBN 0 7182 2953 3

Printed in Great Britain by Springbourne Press Ltd